Kicking Against the Pricks

Kicking Against the Pricks © 2013 by Stephen M. Wilson

Published by Raw Dog Screaming Press
Bowie, MD

First Edition

Cover art: Steven Archer
Cover design: Jennifer Barnes
Book design: M. Garrow Bourke
Editor: Stephanie M. Wytovich

Printed in the United States of America
ISBN 978-1-935738-55-8
Library of Congress Control Number: 2013951962

www.rawdogscreaming.com

Acknowledgements

Artifact: Green Girl, "of Winter and light", Secret Estate Sale

Avante-Garde for the New Millennium (Raw Dog Screaming Press): Fibonacci, Slow Burn

Black Box: Keep Tahoe Blue

Black Petals: The Exiles

Bondage –Tales of Obsession (Sam's Dot Publishing): Phantasia!

Dark Duet (dkhdk): Strangers in this Place

Connections (Peace and Justice Network): The Injudicious Prayers of Pombo the Idolater (under the tile "Pombo finds his Waterloo")

Doorways: The Plainfield Ghoul, Alt. Hist. Anagram, Dec. 24th

Everyday Weirdness: Coventry

Goreletts: The Brood vs. The Oompa Loompas, Soft belly babies

Hungur: Goin' South, Clay and the Skimmer

Microcosms: "Märzen, sauerkraut and… "

Paper Crow: I, Cannibal, Angel's Den

poetsespresso newsletter: Icky, Lime Ricky, Love hurts, "Cinquain for October", "simultaneously reading", DOG

PunkHorror.com: Betty Rage (as a podcast)

The Queer Collection (Fabulous Flash Publishing): Death in the Streets of Fair Verona

SARM: Candy

Scifaikuest (Sam's Dot Publishing): "Forsaken sigh", "Four arms explore my body", Trophy Kill

SCI FI FAN II: First Contact

Shadow Box: Blue Moon

The Shantytown Anomaly: "Snipped, clipped and cut"

Star*Line (Science Fiction Poetry Association): Howard *d'oeuvres,*

Sun Shadow Mountain: "faith alone"

Wicked Karnival Sideshow Press: Wicked Carnival: A Tribute to Tod Browning Jr., The Story of Little Wet-the-bed, Swallowed!

contents

Introduction: KICKIN' IT
by Linda D. Addison

STEPHEN ON WHAT he looks for in a poem:

Well I like unique perspectives and, like with traditional haiku, ideas that juxtapose each other—this often works as a sort of "twist ending"— you think that the piece is about a specific subject and then that kireji pops in and you're sent somewhere else entirely.

From Six Questions For.. blog interview by Jim Harrington

You hold a book of fiction and poetry in your hands, by Stephen M. Wilson. You may wonder why this title, *Kicking Against the Pricks*? Anyone who has read Stephen's work or knew him understood he was a samurai writer. Stephen was fearless and honest in listening to the universe, dripping its dark song to the world, making shapes with words. From "love hurts"

life-blood o
      o
       z
      i
   bet n ween
    fin g ers

i come to you
heart in
hand

Stephen passed May 22, 2013 after a long battle with cancer. This collection was born after Stephen attended the 2012 World Horror Convention/Horror Writers Association in Salt Lake City, Utah. We met there in hopes of finding a publisher for *Dark Duet*, a poetry collection we wrote together.

Energized when he returned home, Stephen told me he was putting together his first solo collection. I was excited to see what he would create because I loved Stephen's writing. No matter how deep the emotion, how dark the subject, Stephen wrote with complete abandonment, giving everything to the poem or story, not flinching from shadowed corners. I admired and loved that quality in his writing, especially since I also would rather see painful truth then look away.

Creating *Dark Duet* with him was a life-changing experience for both of us. We couldn't be more different on the outside, but somehow we found, through writing together, a deep connection on the inside. Reading *Kicking Against the Pricks* brought into clear focus Stephen's compassion for anyone hurt, his willingness to show us the wounds. There are stories of abuse and its real or supernatural repercussions.

What is the measurement of his life? Stephen wrote poetry, fiction, interviewed authors, loved being an editor (for the joy of giving authors an opportunity to be read). His twitterzine, *microcosms*, was created to exclusively publish short speculative poetry. Stephen was a scholar, and loved to explore different poetry forms. There is work here that reflects a thought-provoking mix of religion and science-fiction. In "First Contact" he combines the concept of a virgin mother and aliens: Ascension? Asuncion? Try abduction!

How do we measure the depth of an author's commitment to writing? Stephen loved to be an author and editor and enjoyed playing with words, sometimes invoking smiles:

Märzen, sauerkraut and …
braaains!
Zombie Oktoberfeast

From someone else who loved Stephen deeply:

In this world there are many artists that follow the guidelines in any performing, as well visual arts. Stephen M. Wilson, my lover, my companion, my best friend, was and will be the exception in mastering and breaking the guidelines in the English Language. From his short horror stories, to his haiku, Stephen gave a little of himself with each piece he wrote. To see my companion work hard for long periods of hours on his writing was like seeing an artist giving us a view of his soul, in little quantities. These little quantities helped capture, as well as inspire many writers, editors, but most importantly me.

As a dancer I have learned, from my husband's writing, to capture my feelings more through my dance, as my Stephen did with his words. I will forever admire, respect, but especially miss him. His laughter was contagious, the little twinkle in his eyes when he said, "I love you honey"; the sarcastic humor he had towards life. These are the qualities that I see in my husband, through my eyes.

Thank you, Adrian Wilson Junez...

From me to Stephen, using the titles of his work (I'd like to think he would approve):

Kicking it, even when Love Hurts,
    Goin' South to Keep Tahoe Blue
"simultaneously reading" Fibonacci
    on the Soft Belly of Babies.

I, Cannibal, have no Sympathy for the Devil
    even as "Four arms explore my body",
Pricks, "snipped, clipped and cut"
    let others sing of Death in the Streets of Fair Verona
while Bloody Mary and Betty Rage refuse to let hope die
    even as they swallow the Clay and the Skimmer.

Kicking ==|Against
    them
    all of them...

How to measure a writer's life? Is it the number of words in print, the number of poems, stories, interviews? *Kicking Against the Pricks* is over 16,000 words. Stephen never had a website, although he had an active Live Journal site. I'm compiling his work for a Wikipedia page that I hope will be filled in by others who have published his work or been edited by Stephen.

Stephen was authentic in his love of writing, editing, and all things that had to do with writing. Few people can do all this well, but he did. Writing was Life for him and he was fearless in singing the song of this life. When he was too sick to travel Stephen said now he had more time to write.

So go ahead, jump into Stephen's first and last work shaped by his own hand. If he was courageous enough to face the world without flinching, you can read it, and laugh, sigh, be entertained, be touched. This is the world, raw and beautiful, through the unique mind of Stephen M. Wilson.

—Linda D. Addison, August 2013

...why persecutest thou me? it is hard for thee to kick against the
pricks.
Acts 26:14, The Bible, KJV

The Exiles

Your aura of complex distance
spun my web of felicity.
The Sado-Masochistic waltz
danced between you and me
ended. I felt, I heard, I saw—
a feather, a robin, a rose,
as the tranquil tempest wavered—
settled—my heart's repose
commenced. I screeched! I laughed! I moaned!—
At penal, penile quarantine,
as He cast us two, me with you
(my foil) in this scene—
our life. Jilted! Naked! Ashamed!
My lips belied my mind—my heart.
Now cipher, zephyr and pathos—
Eden we must depart.

First contact

A virgin mother is hard to believe
    Or the talking serpent who deceived Eve
There is a logical explanation
    'Others' once used Earth as a space station
Think it over it's not hard to conceive
    Angels, Aliens—what do names matter?
Jacob saw beings descend from a ladder
    Lowered from a spaceship not the sky
More was out of joint there than just his thigh
    Fought God? (Who was he trying to flatter?)
And then there was Sodom & Gomorrah
    Laser beams shot from the ship Pandora?
Same when the walls of Jericho came down
    A ship could easily have felled a town
There are more examples, a plethora.
    Ezekiel saw wheels within more wheels
From a fiery spaceship with two keels
    Looking like men, stepped four odd beings

With four faces, hooves and two sets of wings
    Sounds like they were from the planet Voncreels
That trick with the parting of the Red Sea
    Sounds like the doings of ETs to me
With a massive fan they dried it just right
    Don't forget the cloud by day/fire by night
I wonder what in the world *that* could be?

Elijah, *twice,* summoned fire from the sky
On a 'chariot', away he did fly
　　It sounds nothing like the style of God
More like he had his own personal pod
　　Flaming chariots are too hard to buy
Mary's son Jesus was the construction
　　Of alien/human reproduction
Where have you been? Newsflash at eleven—
　　They both levitated into Heaven?

Ascension? Asuncion? Try abduction!
　　So Voncreelians inspired The Book
And superstition was their perfect hook
　　They figured out that we humans were dense
Come on think about it, it just makes sense
　　Just open your mind, take another look
There was no Immaculate Conception
　　Nor was there a speaking snake's deception
A virgin mother is hard to believe
　　Or that talking serpent who deceived Eve
First contact was the Bible's inception.

KEEP Tahoe Blue

DELORES WHITMORE RETCHED and then tossed the gore-slicked fishing lure, a chunk of her bloodied left eye dangling from its sharp tip, into the water.

She then reached one gloved hand into her camel Prada bag for a hanky to stymie the blood and simultaneously grabbed for the Glock securely holstered in a red lace garter hidden beneath the hem of her DKNY skirt.

With revenge burning cold in the frigorific blue of her remaining eye, she peered around the deserted, twilight darkened shore of Lake Tahoe.

"You're going to regret fucking with me, Vince Cappelli," she said under her breath before repeating the chant, "Ph'nglui mglw'nafh Cthulhu R'lyeh wgah'nagl fhtagn!"

The surface of the blue water quavered.

simultaneously
reading Torah *and* Tao
     Hadopelagic soul

Trophy Kill

stuffed head framed by wings
mounted in the den
Jon's first Angel Hunt

BlOOdY MaRY

SISTER FUCK WAS eleven when the Blessed Virgin appeared to her.

Growing up, she had been regaled with stories of her mother's and two aunts' own sightings (often by her uncle, Father Kohlberg). Her mother, the oldest of the three, had spotted Jesus grinning at her from a pile of Kraut that now sat shellacked and proudly displayed beneath the glass counter at Messiah Brauhaus (so renamed *after* the miraculous appearance).Aunt Ursula, the odd middle child, swore that she's been visited by the Buddha who she claimed had told her to pawn her 2-karat & platinum wedding set to buy a plane ticket, leave her husband and seven children and move to Burma, while Aunt Corinna, like herself, had seen the Blessed Virgin (although Francesca and Ursula always dismissed their youngest sister's claim as unreliable since the visitation had only been in a dream).

None of her matriarchs' sightings, though, had had the *stigmatic* quality of Sister Fuck's Immaculate Inception—Mary had literally sprung from her uterus.

And now, after nearly thirty years with The Sisters of Perpetual Bliss, even with the knowledge of the unfortunate, nasty little nickname the other nuns called her when they thought she was out of earshot, her faith was as strong as ever.

She smiled as the image of the Holy Mother, now brown and crusted with age, serenely gazed down upon her from the Maxi-pad nailed to her convent cell wall.

Angel's Den

The golden-green
scales of seraph wings
glisten in the nebulous
depths of the angel's
den.

A lamina blanketing
centuries of grizzled
bones sucked dry of their
marrow and the fresh rot of
carrion corpses.

A familiar fetor of fear
emanates from the
new quarry
exciting Gabriel
to erection.

Shimmers of a lurid grin
expose barbed teeth
which he sinks into the
tender white belly
of the child.

Faith, alone,
Cannot move mountains
But faith and a warhead …

Forsaken sigh
From Crucifix
Marooned by Mothership

Pica

... went to market

"HI GALS!"

Maggie sets her keys on the Formica table and drops into the vinyl booth across from Leslie and Nina. They have been meeting at this little diner in Portland ever since she married Matt and moved from Georgia to Oregon. After nearly seven years, she still has not gotten used to going from Ms. Corvidae to Mrs. Corvidae-Black.

Nina looks at Maggie's keys with delight. "You've still got it!"

"Got what?"

"The Buddha Buddy." Nina picks up the keys and brandishes the statue for the others to see. "I nearly forgot about this little fellow. It's been months"

"Three months and two days, to be exact," Maggie replies. "That was the day I found out I was...*expecting.*"

"Oh my god!" Leslie, the only one of the three who is already a mother, says. "You will make a great mom, hon."

"A baby. Oh, Mag, I've prayed for this. What does he think?"

"Oh you know Matt. He's wanted a son for a long time." Maggie lies.

"We've got to throw you a shower! Invite Laura-Louise and Minnie and...what's your neighbor's name?"

"Mrs. Sabatini."

"Yeah, Mrs. Sabatini. And the Fiddlers!"

They all laugh. Maggie has played the fiddle since childhood. When she moved to Eugene, she discovered and eventually joined Ye

Olde Oregon Fiddlers.

"What a hoot that will be," Nina says. "Mrs. Sabatini and all those fiddlers in the same room."

"At least your kid will be part of the Toobychubbies generation," Leslie says, "instead of that horrid purple dinosaur."

"Hey," Nina says, "You know there's a great baby boutique just down the street."

They finish their lunch and walk to the boutique.

Instead of the expected pinks and blues, the dominate colors of the store are pale yellow and sea green. Maggie rubs a green blanket against her cheek. It reminds her of the one wrapped around Matt. Across the aisle is a small turnstile adorned with various jars and tubes. She picks up a small flat jar. The label reads: "EeWahKee: The-Mud-That-Heals." She turns it in her hands a moment before reading the warning: "Consult your physician before adding clay to your diet."

Your diet? She puts it back and picks up a larger bottle. Its label is more blatant: "Down Home Georgia White Dirt," which triggers memories of her childhood friend, Kaolin Butler. She walks to the counter.

Nina and Leslie join her.

"Whatcha find?" Nina asks, craning to see what Maggie is buying.

"Organic clay. Thought I'd give myself a facial to celebrate."

They part ways, Maggie promising to send Nina a list of guests to invite to the shower.

During the drive home, Maggie opens the jar and scoops some of the thick clay out with two fingers. She studies it a moment before popping some into her mouth.

It tastes a lot better than the soil she has been eating for the past several weeks from Matt's grave in the backyard.

...stayed home

Maggie, at the bedroom mirror, said, "It...*she* would be growing in me by now. We could try again. I could cancel tonight."

"Don't want any kids," Matt said and then took another sip of Jack Daniel's from the wine glass. "At least not if I have to fuck you to get 'em."

He laughed.

"We both know I never had the right equipment for you to begin with," she said as she set the lipstick down next to her keys and gazed at the Buddha keychain.

"That's what they call callin' the kettle black ya fat lesbo!"

"You're not getting any younger yourself... "

The half-filled glass connected with the side of her head. Whiskey doused her as shards of glass followed her descent to the carpet.

"Consider tonight canceled." He picked up her fiddle and smashed it against the wall. "And no more hangin' out with those two Stepford dykes you're always runnin' off to see."

She lay there and cried as Matt sauntered away. The glass hurt, but the pain was mild compared to the beating she received the night she told Matt they were expecting. The night he beat the baby out of her.

She'd told everyone that she tripped and fell down the stairs and was lucky that she hadn't broken her neck.

"The baby...he can't do that to...to *us*." She placed a hand on her stomach. "I won't let him hurt you...again."

She struggled to stand. Her head was swimming, but anger and a maternal instinct motivated her. She picked up the remains of her ruined fiddle and stumbled through the house in Matt's wake.

She found him in the den, passed out in his ugly brown recliner, just as expected. She stared at her husband a moment and then shoved the jagged wooden end of the fiddle's neck into his neck. She pushed until the end was buried deep in brown tweed. Matt's eyes shot open and his right hand locked like a vice around her wrist trying to pull the wood from his neck as his life blood spurted everywhere. Eventually his grip lightened and his head lolled forward. The flow turned into a trickle.

She remembered a quote from her favorite book: "Husbands die every day."

…had roast beef

I shove a fistful of the moist soil into my mouth and suck on it.

This is what I remember, as I sit on Matt's grave.

My mother died when I was seven years old and my father remarried. The evil fairytale stepmother made me into the magpie who nests at the foot of the cliff. And my sister, she made into a cuckoo. Every Saturday at noon the cuckoo lays an egg in my nest.

"Ya know," Kaolin said, "It's okay to eat it." We'd found the clay deposits a few weeks earlier near an abandoned mine outside of Augusta.

"Oh?" I wasn't really paying attention, concentrating instead on the warmth and dampness radiating through her thin cotton dress as she pulled a silver comb through my hair.

"Ma says that Great Gran was eatin' it since she was smaller 'an me," she said. "Lets in God."

She held the comb in front of my face. "There. All done."

I lifted my head from her lap and looked at her. Kaolin Butler was 'black as the Ace of Spades' (one of Daddy's phrases) and she was the most beautiful person I had ever seen.

"We gotta get undressed, though. Do a proper ritual."

I thrilled at those words.

I've never told this tale before, but I will tell it to you. I was thirteen years old when my stepmother died. She changed me into a magpie and I plucked out her eyes.

"You been hangin' out with that dirty nigger again." Stepmonster's back hand came with lightning speed. "What have I told you about that Butler girl?" She hit me again.

My nose filled with blood, blocking the strong smell of catfish which'd been frying on the Wedgewood a few inches away.

Later, my eye swelled and turned shades of purple and black.

"You know what your daddy's gonna—"

I grabbed the handle of the skillet and swung it at her. The sound the cast iron made as it connected with her head was almost as satisfying as the half-gurgle, half-scream she'd released as she dropped to the linoleum, her hands clutching at her face as it was cooked off by hot grease.

Every Saturday, the cuckoo comes to me, takes my head, and lays it on her knees. With a silver comb she strokes my hair as she talks of the sea.

"Your pa won't ever find out," she'd said. "No one ever come out here and look for 'er, just assume she ran off. Now you can go live with that aunt on the West Coast."

"I can't leave you," I'd said, rising quickly from her lap. "I love you." I'd held her soft brown face, the skin silky between blistered hands. "We're in love!"

"You know it ain't gonna work," she said. "Two girls, one *black* and one *white*. They'd kill us."

"But... "

"No more now. You gonna go to Oregon and have a proper upbringin'. I'm gonna stay here. One day, we both be married, *this* nothin' but a long buried memory."

We'd made love the afternoon we buried my stepmother. That was the last I ever saw Kaolin Butler. Two weeks later, Daddy shipped me off to his sister's in Oregon.

A memory long buried.

I sit on my late husband's grave, the taste of fresh earth on my tongue.

I am the magpie. Maggie the magpie. I have slain the knight and there she did burn. I am Maggie. I am the cuckoo.

...had none

Imagine you have good news—the best news in the world—and the person you most looked forward to sharing that news with beats the crap out of you.

You know every man wants to be a father.

Now imagine you're a married woman in your mid-thirties and, after years of marriage, you haven't produced any kids—no heir for your husband to boast about, to call junior, to toss a ball around with.

Think about how happy you'd be if your gynecologist told you you're pregnant. All those years, enduring his pale little worm and finally...you're ecstatic. You're already beginning to glow. You spend the afternoon with your two best girlfriends, but you keep the pregnancy a secret. You almost slip and tell them, but he should be the first to know. After lunch, you cut your usual shopping trip short. You want to return home early and prepare a special dinner to deliver the news over.

You cook his favorite, a roast with new potatoes and string beans and a chocolate cake made from scratch, not a box.

You wait for the perfect moment to tell him, across the candle-lit dinner table.

"Matt, I'm pregnant."

You watch him freeze, three string beans impaled on a fork halfway between the plate and his mouth.

"What did you say?"

"We're going to be parents." You beam at him.

He rises from his chair and slowly walks toward you. You've been waiting for this moment for years. The hug. The tears. The joy.

Instead, a backhand across the face knocks you, and your chair, to the ground. Then a kick in the stomach and another and another.

You black-out.

You wake-up; every inch of your body is in pain.

You're in a hospital with a concussion.

The doctor tells you about this break and that fracture and how lucky you are that the fall down the stairs didn't break your neck.

"And, oh yes," he says, "I'm so sorry, but you lost the baby."

You're in shock, and you don't correct the doctor when he repeats your husband's lie about falling down the stairs. Besides, even though the drinking has increased, your husband never hit you before.

Then one night, he hits you again. You know some people accept this kind of abuse their whole lives. But you make sure that he never hurts you, or the baby that is growing inside you (for now you know that the hospital lied), again.

You know what to do. You've done it before. Afterward you bury the body and convince people he's out of the country on business. Matt works for himself and has no real friends, so you know the story will hold at least until the birth.

You bury your spouse and then, almost as an afterthought, you eat some of the soil from his grave. It becomes a ritual.

Eventually you forget it's a grave. You forget the doctor not only told you your baby died, but that your insides were so messed-up from 'the fall', you'll never be able to carry a child to term. You forget all as you feel her growing inside you.

…went wee, wee, wee, all the way home

They sit there as always, Nina prim and proper in a pink hound's-tooth shirt, short dark hair slicked back and shiny. Leslie in a tie-dye shirt and blue jeans, long straw hair in a twist. They both smile at her as she approaches their booth for the final time.

"Look at that Buddha belly!" Leslie says

Nina says, "Honey, you don't look so well. When was the last time you saw Dr. Levin?"

"Everything's fine." Maggie says, although the pain in her stomach has become almost unbearable. "Just one more week."

Tension hangs in the air as they eat their lunches in relative silence.

Maggie is sad that this will be the last time she sees her friends.

I'm going to be a mother, she thinks. *A new life. The former things have passed away.*

They say their goodbyes.

She feels as if her womb is filled with brimstone and broken glass. The need to urinate dominates her whole existence. Pee—every time she sits to pee only a trickle allows itself to be released and then ten minutes may pass and she has to go again—trickle, push, trickle, strain, pain. Always the same. And the constipation—the last time she sat on the toilet she felt her rectum tear as she pushed. She watched with fading vision as the blood-tinged water swirl within the bowl and disappear. That was nearly two days ago. She has stopped eating everything but the clay and is now nearly blind. She has endured worse in her life and all that matters now is the baby. Then, her water breaks, oozing down between her thighs instead of gushing. She strips off her thin slip and waddles naked toward the den. Slowly, exploring each step with her toes, she descends. At the bottom of the stairs, she counts five steps and then leans slightly forward and pats at the air until her hand encounters the rough tweed of Matt's recliner. She bends a little more and grips both arms of the chair with sweaty hands. She tries to block out the pain.

Squatting, more goo oozes from her swollen flaps. Pushes. Screams. Pushes. Sweats. Screams. Pushes some more. Push. Push. Push! Her lips stretch.

Moments later, she drops into the rough chair.

"Momma's little piggy hungry?" she asks, bringing the wriggling slimy thing toward her. In one swift motion, it strikes, savagely lopping-off her breast.

Dedicated to NKH

Kicking Against the Pricks

I

1

US

wee

child

wren fly

Heaven Bound!

love soar; feat/wing.

Angel-birds dive; surface breaking

Ordered pair, Matter/Anti-matter: Morning Glory Mantra

Phoenix ashes dust snail-shell—COCO-DE-MER
A kiss from pomegranate lips betrays my blame.

Me why? Know—not the powers of three-9—
Blame not my y—broken X, fault umbilical of
Chi Lotus. Phallus not my choosing (though would)!
I also ROAR!

Calculate: X+X=SHE…is woman/princess; Frog prince, I?
Kiss, or catch a fly? Fly children, we won! Fly child, wee one—
Burst forth flowers of dawn!
Choose Man. Fly Phoenix, burst like Sunflower from Hell—Heaven
bound
Betray not, my lips.

Death smiles, patient of Nature's patterns
Ordered pair, Adam/Eve…do Angels matter?
Back is breaking; feet sore. A rib strayed from my side
Heaven bound but cannot fly!
Wretched children, we/us/one/me
BETRAYED!
Days numbered like Fibonacci.

SIOW BUrn

In a Pollock Rorschach
of imagination
the blood-egg burst
and the beast
looses its heart beat

I swim to the surface
of the pink embryonic sea
the cutting of new teeth
are sharp against cord
loosening it from Adam's apple pi

Is this the mathematical equation
of an iconoclast—
tasting your soul, blacked
and crisp, yet
lazy like a summer breeze?

I rise through moist flames
origami phoenix
twisting and turning in upon myself
as my other me pulsates
losing a soul that is now mine.

Stephen M. Wilson

Knuckle-hook and collarbone

As locked belly rhythm
Soils naked hearts
Writhing
Grinding
And swinging hammers numb
Wetly open parts
Erecting
Blinding
She is red

As machine tastes thumb
Spine spurts marrow
Satanically
Unctuous
And memory squeals wire
Thousands slip, swallow
Tightly
Scrumptious
I am mad

As denuded zombies worm
Collecting skin, hair
Dragging
Fitting
And squalid babies gleam
Insides soft, rare

Soiling
Splitting
He is dead

Betty Rage

"JUDAS FUCKING PRIEST!" from behind glossy red lips.

He reaches for the button-panel, fingertips grazing a pert nipple encased in paten-leather.

"Sorry," he mumbles.

"Another damned black-out," she responds, as she fumbles in her pocket-book and retrieves a small cell phone.

"Who you gonna call?" he asks as she flips open the phone. The green glow lights up her face.

"Fuck!" she closes the Razor.

"You okay?" he asks, not really caring as he ogles her from head to toe. *'Freakdeaky,'* he thinks, *'just like the last one'*. He always had a thing for the weird chicks, and this one, with her ass length raven hair, complete with extremely short bangs, metal studs and hoops protruding from all over her milky-skinned face, and outrageous clothing that looked like a cross between a Catholic schoolgirl and a dominatrix, fit the bill perfect.

"Important appointment," she says almost absentmindedly while putting the phone back in her bag.

"They'll understand. Power'll be back on soon."

After nearly a year of therapy, he had resolved not to do it again, but this bitch provoked him with her fuck-me-red-plaid Catholic schoolgirl skirt.

He 'accidentally' gropes her chest again, this time lingering for a moment longer, and then pulls away when she tenses.

He can't help himself. He moves in, pressing his swelling crotch against her hip as he pushes her into a corner and hurriedly unzips.

Her fishnets get ripped as they struggle.

She bites off a chunk of his lip as he covers her mouth in a forced kiss.

His blood and saliva mingle on her tongue.

"Wha…what?" he stammers. He is sprawled on the floor, his legs jutting out at unnatural angles. He gazes upward, confused by their sudden change in positions.

She is transformed—larger, more muscular.

She bends over him and tears his pin-striped shirt open. Tortoise-shell buttons fly in every direction.

She shoves large, meaty fingers under the elastic of the boxers that peak from beneath his unzipped slacks. With one quick motion, she rips both pieces of clothing from him, exposing his quickly shrinking erection.

"What the…" he turns on his stomach and tries to scurry away but in the confined space and with two broken legs, it is futile. His bloody lip quivers as he looks over his shoulder at her.

With his tattered pants still gripped in her fist, she plants both hairy, large-knuckled hands on her hips like Wonder Woman and leers at him.

Movement beneath her skirt draws his attention away from her eyes for a moment.

"What the fuck," he babbles looking once again into her eyes, "I'm…I'm sorry. Okay!"

A deep laugh resonates from her throat.

"Just don't…don't hurt me," he pleads.

A thick tentacle pokes out from beneath the hem of her skirt and begins to sway through the air towards him.

"Oh my god," escapes his lips as he realizes what it is.

He stares, dumfounded, as the sinewy penis, at least three feet long and nearly six inches around, dances in front of his face like a cobra.

He tears his gaze from the monstrosity and looks again into her eyes. "Please…"

Her eyes leave his and move slowly down his body before stopping.

She smiles.

"No." He whispers as the monstrous impossibility stop its manic dance and begins to slither in the direction of her gaze, splattering a sticky trail of hot pre-cum down his back like a slug-trail.

She laughs.

He screams.

Soft belly babies
Two hearts strong rhythm–stiff hooks
Both splitting wetly

Stephen M. Wilson

ICkY, LiME RICkY

Lime Ricky was a mean little tot
'fore Mother killed him and let him rot
    His blood grew ticker
    Turned to green ichor
And his corpse oozes slimy green snot

Sympathy for the Devil

THE DEVIL IS always on the move—he is lost without a map.

Was it not he who rolled the stone from the tomb?

The fruits of his labors include:

Penicillin   &   Astronomy

The apple that fell on Newton's head was the very one discarded by our first parents, giving them awareness of loneliness, leading him to discover gravity.

Now we all know the gravity of loneliness. So we change jobs, religions, friends, lovers—always searching for the snowflake that matches our own.

They say no two are alike—I say they're wrong.

Sun/Moon, God/Satan, Friends/Lovers, all reflections of the other. Our lack of meaningful relationships stems from didactic, left-brain functioning. We have forgotten how to feel—how to see the whole picture, not just the orderly fragments that the left wants to classify as A B & C. What about D?

Devil

We are lonely because we have forgotten to feel. He is lonely because he feels too much.

So the Devil is constantly on the move—going down the snowy slopes, searching for that one snowflake, hoping he will find it before the Son returns to melt the snow.

Green Girl

O proud death,
What feast is toward thine eternal cell…

Hamlet V-II *by William Shakespeare*

SHE AWOKE COUGHING thick muddy water from her lungs. Her eyes were assaulted by darkness. Subtle scents permeated the heavy air; moist smells mixed with the perfume of wildflowers and the fresh scent of newly shaved pine, these scents masked by a dominating pungent odor of recently tilled soil.

She searched her memory for any clues as to where she was, how she had come to be there and, most importantly, *who* she was. Only disconnected fragmented images came; a pair of pale fragile hands stringing bright flowers into a garland, a pair of massive ornate thrones occupied by an equally ornate couple, a pair of familiar intense searching blue eyes and the beautiful young aristocratic face that housed them. This last induced in her both longing and despondency.

"Hey non nonny, nonny…" a snippet of song drifted through her muddled thoughts.

Hands gripped her shoulders, the fingers digging painfully into her tender flesh. She heard a shriek.

"DEATH!" her own voice shrilled in her ears.

She jerked forward slamming her head into a solid wall then watched as multi-colored lights dance before her dazed eyes.

Momentarily she realized that the sensation of restraint and the scream were not of the here-and-now but instead a part of her fledgling memory somehow mysteriously connected to the eyes.

Her fingers, tracing the hard ceiling that was inches from her face, felt smooth polished wood. She explored its surface coming to a corner that angled downward. With dawning dread, she realized where she was.

In the ensuing panic, everything had surprisingly come back to her; the prince's professed love and subsequent rejection, her father's betrayal followed by his untimely death, the royal couple's pity, the madness, the cold embrace of the brook.

It had taken hours of scratching and clawing, her nails one by one peeling back in agony, before she had finally been able to create a fissure in the wood. Gravity had done the rest, the weight of the soft earth above pushing through the crack and splitting the coffin lid into splinters.

It had taken even longer, on quavering legs that caused her bedraggled body to lurch uncontrollably, to reach Kronborg Castle.

I died, yet somehow, whether by miracle or by curse, I live, she thought as her stomach grumbled.

She entered the palace. At the end of a dimly-lit hall, she looked upon the carnage of the scattered corpses of her brother, Laertes, and of Denmark's royal family.

After a moment, Ophelia dropped on all fours to the cold stone floor. She leaned in close to her deceased brother; the only sounds the rasp of her shallow breath and the loud growl of hunger pains. She reached out and brushed at a strand of his auburn hair revealing the pale profile beneath. She leaned in closer and, closing her eyes, inhaled his familiar familial scent. A lone tear escaped the confines of her closed lids as she planted a gentle kiss on his milky cheek. Then slowly, eyes still shut, she parted her lips and took the first satisfying bite.

Stephen M. Wilson

Death in the Streets of Fair Verona

O Romeo, Romeo Fortune's fool
  debate our men-love, self applied
with thousands unknowing
  you took fee-simple of my life!
Oft' thought I, how simple that we
  pricked love for pricking
when thou first whispered
  thy tale against mine hair.
Unknowing, us, in our youths
  the spirits and boys painted nothing harshly
all hautboys undeserving
  of Painter's Palace of Pleasures
And how simple our love, hid in shame when
  vouched you'd stolin' Juliet–feign!
O calm, dishonorable, vile submission
  Have which princess' heart again?
Here's my heart already a sanctuary–
  my body the altered altar at which you
   prayed
A naked masochist, like He of the cross
  still pining for the Salvation of lust
And O that Queen Mab had steered those
  atomi towards another's leisure
Those nights learning pain was such pleasure
  I your knave, friend, lover, slave!
Here's mine prick already a grave

this idly bleeding body still enrag'd!
O simple, bloody mistress–
    unknowing in my youth!
Soft, lucid grave gallant and would
    From olive foot covering restore flesh,
 restore love
As I exit this, my rebellious body, Nature is mute.
    Have we wronged Heaven in our hellish pursuit?
Love me Master, I am brainsick for air
    Forget about our men who debate and stare
Deny Juliet, and that ye be Montague's heir
    Take me in your arm so that I may die there!
O Romeo, Romeo now I'm Fortune's fool
    For loving a boy so beautiful, so cruel
And in the future our men will refute
    Thousands will not know
The True Tragedy of Mercutio and his Romeo
    And like dumb Petrruchio,
History will be mute.

Stephen M. Wilson

DOG

Rover contemplates
why he created Adam
dyslexic

Man DID eat angels food

In the sweat of they face shalt thou eat bread, till thou return unto
the ground;
          So the men sat down, in number about five thousand.
"I will rain bread from Heaven for you."
 And Jesus took the five loaves and the two fishes, and looking up to
Heaven, he blessed, and brake, and gave to the disciples, and the
          disciples to the multitude.
"When I have broken the staff of your bread, ten women shall bake
you bread in one oven and ye shall eat the flesh of your sons, and
the flesh of your daughters shall ye eat."
      Take. Eat: this is my body."
The bread of tears, the bread of wickedness, the bread of idleness,
      the bread of sorrows—it is manna.
Then he said, "Cast your bread onto the water, for
    it is written: 'Man shall not live by
      bread alone'."

Stephen M. Wilson

I, cannibal...

…will
sniff you out
in the jungle of
N I G H T
cuff you with
         blue
tongue nostrils
chew toes
         onebyonebyone
lap moisture from
crevices/arches/pits/sockets-scarlet
  all those hairy acrid spaces
suck marrow
from all   g
bone   r
weight each   e
pungent   y
morsel with
         hands
           lips
        teeth

nipplesnosecockthumbsballsack

beyond
  L O V E

beyond
    L U S T

a hunger
insatiable

I, Cannibal
will
devour
you

Stephen M. Wilson

THE BROOD VS. THE OOMPA LOOMPAS

Can chocolate soothe the savage mom?

WHEN CHARLIE DUMPED her after finding a Golden Ticket and subsequently inheriting Willie Wonka's factory, Nola went mad. Now she sits in Somafree birthing an army of rage in the form of small ski-jacket clad demons. Will the Oompa Loompas be able to defend Charlie's Chocolate Factory from The Brood?

Four arms explore my body
our six legs, entwined
Vitruvian Man

Virtual Pair: The Final Peril

> He that dippeth his hand with me in
> *the dish, the same shall betray me.*
> —Matthew 26 KJV

"NO!" SHE SHRIEKED, struggling against the ropes that bound her to the chair—not silken ties but rough twine, not cushions of velvet or satin but hard straight-backed wood.

"Please, please, please…not again!"

The walls and floor of the dank room were gray cement with mold growing halfway up the wall. Here and there large roaches would scuttle across the corrosive surface. Slimy rivulets, the color of sickness, hung from the low, claustrophobia-inducing ceiling, occasionally dripping like chicken gristle. The corpses of her would be rescuers lay piled in a dark corner, reduced to nothing more than a rotting hill of offal mobbed by ants.

The girl mewled incoherently and kicked over her chamber pot. It had not been emptied in hours? Days?—time had lost all meaning as she languished in a near phantasmagoric state.

A foul odor permeated throughout the small, cave-like chamber—urine, feces, sweat, and the sour stench of fear. In the past few weeks her jumpsuit had become tight around her waist and breasts. Its pink leather was dirty and straining at the seams, a few of which had become unraveled exposing bits of bruised flesh including one raw nipple the color of roses that he never wooed her with. Now voluptuous, she was a grotesque caricature of her quondam youth.

One of the henchmen grabbed the back of her chair and slowly dragged her toward the dining room—'the bad place'as her regressing mind had come to think of the room—as the other watched and grinned at her luridly.

Physically it was like any other room of its type with a large oak table surrounded by six nondescript chairs, an old oak china cabinet where various mismatched dishes could be seen through its two beveled-glass doors, and a copy of Leonardo da Vinci's *The Last Supper* hanging on one wall. What made it 'the bad place' was not its appearance, but what transpired there, what was about to happen again.

No champagne awaited her. No incandescent candlelight to give the room a soft glow. Instead, standing at the head of the table, was her once obese captor. As always, he hid behind a mask. He thought himself sly, sneaky, but she recognized his husky sensual voice, his musky masculine scent, his brusque touch.

No caviar awaited her. No truffles. No aphrodisiacal oysters. Just the bucket.

"Once again," the now skeletal echo of her demented dream lover demanded of his bound prisoner. Gripping the spoon in his claw, he dipped it into the bucket then inched it, lard-laden, toward her mouth.

"But why lil' ol' moi?" she pleaded, struggling against the ropes.

"Why? Why!…Quantum Mechanics, that's why!' he replied, gazing into her scratched driving goggles, "Every bit of matter produces a corresponding bit of anti-matter. That is why, my dear. Soon I'll be absolute!" He shoved the spoon into her mouth.

As the slick, pallid substance oozed down her throat, Pauline closed her eyes in prayer, not to God above, for he had offered no succor in this, her time of need, but instead in ardent yearning for one touch, one amorous word from the man in the purple mask, her guardian for so many years. She prayed ardently for one fervent, erotic moment. She prayed for rapture.

In return, no dithyrambic lamentations of love whispered in her ear, no sonnets recited, not even the firm chastisement of a Master to his wayward masochist, only indifference as he laughed, "I swore I'd ultimately get you. Ah ha haaaa!"

The Injudicious Prayers of Pombo the Idolater

with help from Lord Dunsany

How you have fallen from heaven, O morning star, son of the dawn! You have been cast down to the earth, you who once laid low the nations! You said in your heart, "I will ascend to heaven; I will raise my throne above the stars of God; I will sit enthroned on the mount of assembly, on the utmost heights of the sacred mountain. I will ascend above the tops of the clouds; I will make myself like the Most High." But you are brought down to the grave, to the depths of the pit.

—Isa 14:12-15 (NIV)

POMBO THE IDOLATER prayed to Mammon and was miffed when his prayer was not instantly answered. So Pombo, in sincere supplication, prayed to Dream for the overthrow of Mammon, an idol friendly to Dream. This was an affront to the propriety of the pantheon. Dream refused to grant his simple prayer. Addled, Pombo anxiously sent ardent adulations to all the ancient idols. The entire repertoire of the revered icons, old and new alike, snubbed Pombo's supplications. By the time he reached the 11th, he began to fear a conspiracy against him.

In the maelstroms of midwinter, Pombo haunted the streets of Washington D. C. praying to a variety of American idols—from the Lincoln Memorial to The Washington Monument, hoping that someone, anyone, would acknowledge his sincere need. He was often seen pressing his pudgy goateed face against the windows of tourist shops filled with every form of gaudy bauble, from clocks featuring

56

Queen Elizabeth or Princess Diana to copper-painted lead Eiffel Towers, plastic Buffalo Nickels a foot in diameter, and 10 inch resin miniature Abe Lincolns, many of these new gods made in Hong Kong, China, and/or India, in chaste communion, until the cops commanded that he clear out. He cruised thrift shops, flea markets, bazaars, and the occasion patio sale looking for some small forgotten statuette, some calm, cross-legged celestial being chiseled from Concubine Red Granite or Chinese Green Marble, that he hoped would be honored to be honored by his honest adulation. Inevitably, he would return to his office with sandalwood that he would subsequently set ablaze in a brazier before beseeching, with idle idylls, minute minor idols of his own.

I have no clue as to whether he was aware of the propriety of the icons and found it piously haughty in the face of his fervent frenzy, or if he had become so deliriously daft in his devotion that it broke him. Whatever his motivation, Pombo the idolater took the Louisville Slugger (he received this as a gift while illegally fundraising during the All Star Game in Michigan), which he kept securely hidden just inside his front door for security, and in a fit of iconoclastic rage went to town on those he felt were the betrayers of his devotion.

After pummeling his personal pantheon into powder, he left his home and traveled across the Continental US consulting Indians, the Middle East flavor as well as Native Americans—Miwok, Mohawk, Cherokee, and Blackfoot—he even offered a federally unrecognized tribe, the Shinnecocks, a $250 million casino land grant in return for an agreeable god, but all was futile.

He called to the traditional gods of Greece and Rome, giving special attention to Mercury in hopes that the messenger god would carry his prayers to Mount Olympos.

In South Dakota he bowed futilely before Mount Rushmore.

In Arizona, he venerated a burning bush but got no reply. He turned his back on the scorched earth, leaving it to the environmentalists. He even tried enticing Alaskans with the money that they could make opening the Arctic National Wildlife Refuge to oil exploration in return for a totem, any totem that would hear his prayers. In his own home state of California, he offered his constituents a historic World War II-era battleship in hopes of some little bit of information that led to a god looking for devotees. When that failed, he tried divination with a fine stein of ale but only got drunk.

In a moment of inspiration, he authored The Threatened and Endangered Idols Recovery Act, but Congress would hear nothing of it.

He returned home feeling defeated and decreased.

Then, while surfing the World Wide Web, he found a reputable arch-idolater who carved idols out of rare stones, and sent him an email. Following several days of impatiently waiting for a reply from the arch-idolater, he finally received an answer. After admonishing Pombo for destroying his own idols, the arch-idolater explained to him the divine etiquette of deities, and how Pombo had offended, and how no idol in the world would reply to his requests. He told him, though, of one god who would not only grant prays to the otherwise unworthy, but would forgive them of their sin if they but only asked. Then the arch-idolater explained to him of how in the village of World's End, at the furthest end of Dénouement Drive, there was a hole, near a garden-wall that was guarded by luminous beings with flaming swords, that was disguised as a well, but that if he lowered himself over the edge of said 'well', and felt about with his feet until they found a ledge, that said ledge was the top of a long flight of winding stairs that led to the edge of the World. He went on to explain that the steps, which were lit by the faint blue gloaming in which the World spins, led directly to this relatively young god who answered prayers, and how, during descent, he would pass Lonely House and under a bridge that led to a place called Waterloo, and how he must avoid the gate-opener known as Exu or Pan or Set or Enki or Azazel or ha-satan or the morning star.

Stopping first in Tracy to bid farewell to his family, Pombo began his long journey to World's End.

Fourteen years later, Pombo was strolling down Dénouement Drive; but how he contrived to get there…I will only say he had become an influential insider susceptible to the enticements and temptations of power. And Pombo found everything just as the arch-idolater had described, and he imagined that the gods were laughing at him through the mouth of the arch-idolater as he gripped the edge of the 'well' feeling around with his feet for the ledge, which after a few moments he found. Pombo descended the steps. There, sure enough, was the gloaming in which the world spins, and the stars shone far off in it faintly; there was before him as he went downstairs but that strange blue waste of gloaming, with its multitude of stars and comets plunging through it on outward journeys and comet returning home. And then he saw the lights of the bridge that led to Waterloo and beyond. A few moments later he saw the morning star, surrounded by dancing flames in rainbow hues, guarding Waterloo. Pombo was hesitant, but only for a moment, before rushing stealthily past the morning star, who intently watched but did nothing to impede him, and into Waterloo. There he stood a moment.

Pombo spied the god that the others claimed to be of ill-repute, the god that answered the prayers that all of the other gods refused to answer.

The god glowed like the corona of a newly exploded sun as he smiled at him and opened his arms in invitation. In his eagerness to fall in worship at the feet of any god that would accept his prayers, Pombo began to run.

Momentum took over and he overshot his target and plunged off the edge of the World and towards the vastly expanding expanse of self-luminous celestial spheres, where he is still falling today. How apropos that Pombo's last stand was at Waterloo.

I'm Stephen M. Wilson and I endorse this narrative.

Stephen M. Wilson

GOiN' SOUth

The ocean is wild tonight
And I am eaten by strange fires
As I'm flung into the midnight sky
300 miles I must swim—
Erupting into his arms
Amid the garbage I dive and stroke—
I gasp for air
As the party moves on

    Blood is drank
    Scars exchanged—

The faces of

    The Dead appear

At the Frathouse he hazes me

    Beating!
    Pounding!
    Bleeding!

His carnal tattoo marks my flesh
I am haunted night and day
Now I pine for the man in the tower
I pray to him across the void

Bring it to my lips, I beg
And his turbid secretions temporarily soothe

The Burning

Arteries of light pulsate through my being—

Celestial Fires!

A ship trailing a comet, bearing flame
Although it may be the road to Hell
The choice is no longer mine

To him I am a form in wax. By him imprinted,
And within him the power to leave the figure, or disfigure it.

Stephen M. Wilson

Phantasia!

O' pedagogue let's retire
And I'll lash you to the bed
Show what you've taught me of desire
For *my* dark lusts now need fed
Every incantation
You've uttered, I'll mock
And for divination
Teach you with my cock

    Blow, blow augur
    Recite by rote
    Ready your throat
    Gulp me like milk
    Devour me you old starved ogre
    For now *I'm* of sorcerer's ilk!

Yes eld' wizard you are tethered
Your turn to be bound by pain's prick
Long your tortures I have weathered
Worship me—be rapt 'round my prick
Take it to the hilt
Light as a hare's prick
Drain it of its silt

    Blow, blow augur
    Recite by rote

Kicking Against the Pricks

Ready your throat
Gulp me like milk
Devour me you old starved ogre
For now *I'm* of sorcerer's ilk!

You saw me bathing from the shore
Pierced my soul with wise eyes heady
A trusting child shy and tore
Pierced the hole 'fore it was ready
Once innocent and chaste
Virtue you did steal
Laid confidence to waste
Value you did kill

I could stop you
At my leisure
Pain is pleasure!
Tables can turn
Can't you see it? Poor you, poor you,
Now *I'm* Master and *you* must learn

Once your perversions I'd obey
Wish I were a boy once more
And all you've taught would go away
Become naïve as before
Once you had my reverence
Innocence is dead
Grant now my severance
Dour upon our bed

Without heart's blood
You can't please me,
Nor appease me
I'm *your* Master!
I'll thrust deeper, create a flood
And delight as it flows faster!

You're a demonic brood of hell
And our house is tore asunder
Our bedchamber your prison cell
Withered wizard, now I plunder
Now you cannot move
Who will have me now?
I longed for your love
Revenge is my vow

Beg me, Master, to calm you
Rub and balm you,
Hold and kiss you
You think now I could?
Well never!
When you vanish no one will miss you

'tis why I return your flagging
Ha! To me *you* are now ill-hoin'd
No more cabobblish bragging
In pain's pleasure we are now joined
Proved an adept adept

O' turgid goblin
You cared not, when I wept
Now you are sobbing

    Woe now to you
    What can you do?
    Nothing to do
    Your secret name
    Too bad for you
    Yen Sid, I've beat you at your game

Your cries now stifled, ex-master
One less abracadabrant word
You're dying too slow—die faster!
Your pathetic prayers can't be heard
Here I cum, gag you now
I heed you no more
Your death will end our row
And cease this, our sadistic war

    Cock *and* anger spent
    You're Soul's
    Repent, hurry!
    Noctuary
    Lament, spirit
    Your myomancy now Hell-bent
    This mouse will no longer hear it!

Stephen M. Wilson

the stinger—

you complain
of a small p
rick but t
he bee
has lo
st i
ts l
if
e

Snipped, clipped and cut
for years, *Bonsai* Woman
lacks a mouth to scream

BlUe MOOn

JOHNNY VANDAL WAS cursed.

Something akin to the Trojan tragedy of Aeneas mixed with a satanic pact—he had rubbed the wrong Portuguese gypsies the wrong way.

That run-in a decade ago with *those* Azorians resulted in his monthly acquisition of fiendish fur, infernal incisors, and chthonian claws, his palms sprouting mandalas instead of pentagrams.

At tonight's gala, he'd lost the golden scarab that was supposed to lift the curse.

Johnny Vandal was cursed.

His true curse, though, was not his werecreatureness, but his gambling addiction.

The blue neon moon was a shine as he stepped through the casino doors into the night.

"Viva, Las Vegas," he said, and then raised his snout and howled.

Cinquain
for October—
Contains vampires, werewolves,
zombies and serial killers.
Scared yet?

Märzen, sauerkraut and …
braaains!
Zombie Oktoberfeast

WhO KillEd COCk RObiň?

For Every Evil
For every evil under the sun
There is a remedy or there is none.
If there be one, seek till you find it;
If there be none, never mind it.
—Mother Goose

RECENTLY I ATTENDED a symposium for the American Psychiatric Association. Doctor Robin Fell, a prominent forensic psychiatrist was the keynote speaker:

"We are gathered here to discuss the question: 'What is Evil?'"

"What I have is an outline of 26 indicators that could be used to rate the 'evilness' of criminals."

I had been in the shadows of Dr. Fell for several years, often at odds in our opinions of criminality and punishment. As well respected as Robin was, all I could think about him was *a diller, a dollar, a ten o'clock scholar!*

He droned on telling gruesome stories of mothers burning their children, serial killers, and cannibalism.

When I retired to my hotel room, my dreams were wrought with gruesome images. The most vivid of them was partially a childhood memory.

This dream stared a pair of young female twins, Mandy and Molly Grundy, who I knew as a child in the late 1960's. They were identical except for one small detail; Mandy had a curl in the middle of her

72

forehead. One day Mandy gutted her twin with a pair of scissors. When later asked why she did it her reply was:

"My sister, Molly's, guts fell out,
And here's what the hell it was all about
The bitch loved coffee and I tea,
And that was the reason that I murdered she."

In my dream, horrid little Mandy was sitting in the audience at the symposium. Suddenly she flew across the room toward the podium screaming:

"I fuckin' hate thee, Doctor Fell;
I think I'll send you straight to Hell;
Though I know I'll end-up in jail,
It's worth your death, I say, ' Oh well!'"

She whipped a pair of scissors from beneath her frilly apron and did Doctor Fell in, blood and gore splashing those in the front rows inciting many of the prominent psychiatrists present to bouts of vomiting. When she was through, Mandy turned to the audience brandishing the scissors as if a sword. Impaled onto the sharp end was one of Doctor Fell's eyes, a curl of veins dangling from the end that matched the curl on Mandy's forehead.

I woke from the nightmare drenched. I stumbled into the restroom and flipped on the light. What I saw was that I was covered in blood. I stripped off my red sticky pajamas and took a long steamy shower. After sluicing off the evidence, I searched the room and sure enough found a pair of bloodied Fiskars tangled in the sheets.

They tell me that I have suffered from a latent, yet volatile combination of narcolepsy *and* sociopathy.

They say that the two disorders were aggravated by my abhorrence for Dr. Fell and, e*specially*, by his speech the previous afternoon. Suffice it to say, Dr. Fell was found murdered in his room, stabbed over 200 times. Several witnesses saw me leaving his hotel room covered in blood, the gore slicked Fiskars gripped in my fist.

Now I sip tea and contemplate the nature of evil in my cell in an asylum named Pumpkin Shell where they assure me I'll keep very well.

WiCKED CarniVaL: A TOaST tO TOd BroWning Jr.

Once just a choirboy from Kentucky
Your grotesque obsessions with the bizarre
Led to side-shows as a teen, felt lucky
Turned ringleader of the macabre bazaar

'The Hypnotic Living Corpse' for a time
Changed your moniker from Charlie to Tod
'Undertook' *Scenting a Terrible Crime*
Imp of the circus, angel to the odd

Blood on your conscious from the "Ride to Death"
Who knows what you lost on that fateful day
Most likely you breathed innocence's last breath
A murky persistence of memory

From this was born *London After Midnight*
Proved you a sublime (though, supine) auteur
Of the subtleties of madness and fright
Your bastard attempt to bring us Stoker

Two years almost lost all, due to the sauce
But followed your blacklisting tragedy
With our first taste of your personal cross
With the release of *The Unholy Three*

Kicking Against the Pricks

Your definitive mark in '31
Put 'universal' monsters on the chart
At the dawn of the Great Depression
Gave U.S. horror cinema its start

When *Dracula* finally came to the screen
Hardly a cinematic *tour de force*
(For example: see armadillo scene)
But steered our psyches on a darker course

Invited our Ids to your black gala
A real Hungarian (those eyes, that bite!)
The public was introduced to Bella
Glad to join with the children of the night

Finally came *Freaks* your magnum opus
Critics thought a bane to society
Struck American culture an ictus
Brought you much deserved notoriety

Now we the misshapen the distorted
New horror writers sinister and bent
Raise our pens to toast our bequest sordid
And carry on your Grand Guignol pageant

       "We salute you—one of us!"
       "We salute you—one of us!"
       "We salute you—one of us!"
       "We *accept* you—one of us!"

love hurts

life-blood o

       o

        z

       i

   bet n ween

    f i n   g   e r s

i come to you
heart in
hand

The Plainfield Ghoul

Bizarre the scene

> Naked
> Headless
> Inverted
> Cool

Piteous soul

> The disemboweled
> corpse reflects

A tiller-tailor's tools

> Twine & ears
> full of nails

Bile interjects when found

> a trophy to pronounce

> *As fevers cool your wayward soul*
> *Each fear reflects the tiller's tool*
> *Needles, nails, & twine interjects*
> *Or so pronounce the harrowed tales*

Stephen M. Wilson

Dark the tales of baubles

       & costumes
       made of flesh

Vulvas by the ounce (Mother's
silver from the grave)
Two murders fresh

       meat added
       to the store
       (of remains)

Boxes to save

       salt preserve –pickled
       eyes keep watch

       A pound of flesh perhaps an ounce
       The grave mound's soil's fresh
       Not one remains to come and save
       You watch as moonlight wanes

Time passes wanes

       the mystery of
       '57's sadistic crime

Silver screen latch

onto history
Hollywood's
story now

Hopkins on *Time*

    cover
    no more knowledge
    to glean

Legend sows now

    Bates
    Leatherface
    Buffalo Bill
    —starring roles

The crime clinched with the latch
Reduced now to "Once Upon A Time"
You glean what you once did sow
A staring role now victim in this scene

Stephen M. Wilson

Clay and the Skimmer

a found poem from Robert Silverberg's The Son of Man

He dreams: drowned cities of antiquity
Once more concealed.

Tentacles wind around his wrists and waist and neck. A fierce rush of
Activity flutters in his skull.

She lets him briefly grasp her slick, metallic wings as she winds her
legs around
Him.

He drives himself into her depths.

He is pleasure's slave!

Still dreaming of antiquity, his rod expands to fill the heavens. It
burns with

Pure, brilliant fire.

He explodes with sensations!

Rainbow hues sweep and crest and mingle with his fiery seed as it
Trumpets across the Cosmos!

Kicking Against the Pricks

Death is an orgasm…
Infinity can be damp and moist!

Stephen M. Wilson

secret Estate sale

Her infinity
not a sideways 8,
but a silken web
stretched from cane-backed chair
to linoleum

where deliquescent sleep
formed crystalline sex …

Lithe egg-filled sack.

    Faith
    of a spider.

The Story of Little Wet-the-bed

"God damn you've peed to bed again,
I thought I told you that's a sin.
The big fat plumber comes," Sis said,
"To bratty boys who wet to bed.
Do you want to be a eunuch?
'Cause he will pull off your tunic
Then take your disloyal wiener
And burn it off with drain cleaner."
Though her warnings were not subtle
Next morn he woke in a puddle
Like a yellow Shroud of Turin
Was the shape of Conrad's urine
A man ran in, alack! alack!
Followed by his exposed butt-crack.
"I am here!" the fat plumber said
As he grabbed little Wet-the-Bed
"Oh my gosh, you're fat and creepy—
Please sir, don't burn off my pee pee."
Conrad began to scream and cry
As the plumber applied the lye
Now he has no penis or balls
Wears a catheter, stares at walls
His big sister laughed as she said,
"I told you not to wet the bed!"

Stephen M. Wilson

Howard d'oeuvres

Chef Lucinda the *bon vivant* Wiccan
Found delicacies ripe for the pickin'
    On furlough in Innsmouth
    Popped a leg in her mouth
Then cried: "Dagon's kids taste just like chicken!"

Swallowed!

...I shall never sleep calmly again
when I think of the horrors that lurk
ceaselessly behind life in time and
space, and of those unhallowed blasphemies
from elder stars which dream beneath the
sea...

—"The Call of Cthulhu" *H. P. Lovecraft*

Chapter IV

HE WAKES TO the sound of gentle surf and the warm morning sun beating down on his almost bare back. Brushing his long, lank hair from his face, he opens his eyes and sees that he is laying face down on an alabaster beach. He raises himself to a sitting position to take in his surroundings. The beach stretches on for several leagues in either direction and on the far inland horizon, he can see the roof tops of a recognizable city. He tried so hard to avoid this epicurean place, this poison city of madness, and as fate would have it, here he was on its charnel shore.

He turns his gaze seaward. His jaw drops at what he sees. Lying several yards away, half in the surf and half on the beach, is a grotesque malignancy of fantastic nightmare. The monstrosity is the size of a temple and has gulls picking at its green gelatinous flesh; flesh that is covered with parasites. Its anthropoid outline is simultaneously an octopus, a dragon and a human caricature with a tentacled head surmounted on a grotesque and scaly body—sprouting rudimentary wings. The beast looks like a creature that could only have crawled from the thighs of his own mother. Within the mass of pulpy feelers, its massive mouth is ajar all dripping with green ooze and sinister with latent horror. A steaming path of gore putrid with the carcasses of decaying fish and other less describable things oozes from that cavern right to where he sprawls. The very sun of heaven seemed distorted when viewed past the polarizing miasma welling out from the sea-soaked perversion. Then memory hits him like a torrent and the last small vestiges of sanity finally leave him.

Later in the afternoon, villagers begin to gather on the beach to gape at the leviathan.

They have come to revel in the spectacle of your misery, taunts a familiar voice.

Yet the spectators avoid contact with the sallow, bedraggled man who wanders amongst them; maybe it is the fetid smell of vomit and rot that wafts from his body or maybe it is his physical deformities, the twitching third arm barely covered by strips of filthy cloth that dangles from the middle of his chest and the crimson scrotum that is swollen to the size of a pomegranate; whatever the reason, they turn away when he approaches. He is unaware that he looks nothing like the handsome, statuesque man who started this journey only weeks earlier.

He wanders away from the crowd and toward the city that awaits him-towards his destiny.

For over a month, a month of strange days, he wanders the streets of the city raving in delirium.

The end is near, you filthy, diseased heathens, the vile voice insinuates from within.

"The end is near, you filthy, diseased heathens!" The man repeats, at the top of his lungs.

He notices a queerness about the people of the city, whose

predominant color is a grayish-green, though they had white bellies. They were mostly shiny and slippery, but the ridges of their backs were scaly. Their forms vaguely suggested the anthropoid; while their heads were the heads of fish, with prodigious bulging eyes that never closed. At the sides of their necks were palpitating gills, and their long paws were webbed. They hopped irregularly, sometimes on two legs and sometimes on four; their baying voices croaking and jabbering in some hateful guttural patois.

One night he wanders into a dark alley and almost trips over the spread legs of a whore, who sits in the shadows on a mound of ash. She looks up at the man and grins, exposing diseased gums where teeth once hung.

"Honey for my honey," she cackles.

She is in a state of filth that rivals his own; topless, with small breasts that resemble shriveled figs. Her skirt is hiked up around her waist, and with both hands she morbidly and spasmodically claws in epileptic madness at her sex like a mongoose digging in the earth for snakes.

"Manna, for that *special* hunger," she moans luridly while spreading her outer-labia to expose the moist interior of her body; offering it up to the man. She cackles again.

He starts to make his retreat from the alley, uninterested in the offer. One last comment from the harlot follows him.

"Come to mother."

Suddenly something snaps and an old familiar rage boils up inside forcing him to turn back towards the filthy whore.

"That's it, sweetheart. All yours," she croons.

For a brief moment, he sees not the Jezebel, but instead the creamy skin of his mother.

He approaches her.

"That's it my darling," she whispers through crimson lips, "You know how to please mommy." She winks at him and is once more the harlot.

He bends over her and embraces her head with his two normal hands, turning it upwards to face him. She closes her eyes and licks the puss from her scabby lips in expectation. He then swiftly shoves the fist of his third arm up into the waiting maw of her ravenous vulva. It is swallowed all the way to the elbow. She gasps and her eyes fly open.

"Oh, you like it rough," she murmurs. "Give it to momma rough. Come on."

He opens the fist that is buried inside of the woman's dank cave and grabs onto something that feels like a nest of sleeping snakes. His three arms work in unison and in one swift motion; he breaks the whore's neck and withdraws his arm from her wetness, his fist filled with her steaming still pulsating entrails.

Fleas, lice, and all other manner of parasites exit the dying body, avoiding the sizzling blood and acrid urine that spews from her dehiscent cunt, making way for new insects that will soon take their place and make the corpse their home.

He covers her with a piece of nearby tattered sackcloth and walks away.

Another day dawns.

It is time to leave this place, the voice orders him and he turns from her, making his way out of the city to a queer dark precipitous hill a few leagues to its east.

There is no vegetation of any kind on that broad expanse, but only a fine gray dust of ash which no wind seems ever to blow about. The trees near it are sickly and stunted, and many dead trunks stand or lay rotting.

There, under the instructions of the voice, he spends the morning gathering the dead branches with which he builds himself a rough shanty that faces the city. Then, like a true eremite, he plants himself in its shade and spends the remainder of the afternoon begging the voice to leave him alone; let him die.

At dusk, he lies down and falls asleep. When he awakes he notices that, overnight, a *kikayon* has grown from one of the dead branches at the top of his shabby booth. He eats the gourd, which is filled with bitterness and sickness, even the smallest bite inducing disgust. But he knows that it is poison and death will be a boon. He grays and turns brittle then perishes in the night. Within days, he is crawling with worms.

Chapter III

The tempestuous sea swallows him swiftly with its whirling and churning-its weeds wrapping around his calves and wrists and head, pulling him down into its abysmal darkness. He sees bizarre and disturbing objects in the surging water. A smile passes across his face as he starts to lose consciousness because, for once, the voice is quiet.

Thank you, he thinks, and then everything goes black.

As he slowly regains consciousness, the first sensation that he becomes aware of is a slushy nastiness as of a cloven sunfish, a stench as of a thousand open graves. In his childhood, back before the voice had come to rule his life, he had come upon a leper on the side of the road while returning from Joppa with a pot of fresh water.

The man had been curled up in a fetal position wearing only a filthy scrap of cloth around his mid-section. The rest of his naked, exposed body had been covered in scabrous, oozing sores. The boy had stood there a moment, staring at the gaunt man in horrified fascination, wondering if he was dead or alive. He had then set down the clay pot and had snapped a twig off of a nearby bush to prod the bundle of diseased bones. When he had gotten within a foot of the leper and started to poke him, a small sound had escaped what was left of his lips. Thinking the man had spoken, the boy had leaned closer—mere inches—to the man's mouth to better hear what he was saying. Suddenly a loud belch had escaped the depths of the man's gut and erupted right into his face. He had jerked away, but not in time to escape the stench of rot and death that assaulted him. He had thrown up violently and ran home, the pot of water forgotten. In hindsight, he had figured out that the leper had been dead and what had happened that day was no more than the natural gas of decomposition.

The odor he now wakes to is something like that, yet much worse, mixed with the stench of rotting fish and just as he did on that long ago day, he retches several times—bringing up hot, chunky bile and seawater. This purging session goes on for several moments until he is finally reduced to dry heaves. Then the realization strikes him that he is in complete darkness.

He begins moving his fingers along the surface where his aching body lies. What they encounter make no sense to him. Every surface that he touches feels hot, wet and fleshy and there is a broad impression of vast angles, the geometry abnormal and loathsome, something redolent of spheres and dimensions apart from ours. It pulsates beneath his touch as if alive.

He sits up and starts groping the dark space in front of him, leaning to the left and then the right, his hand once again encounters the fleshy surface-a wall of it. He drags his hand tentatively along the bumpy, pulsating wall dumbfounded. Then he begins to cry, for recollection is returning; he had been thrown into the raging sea. He remembers. Then he realizes that he must be dead and this, his hell.

How long the hot tears chased each other down his dirty face; it could have been minutes or days. What finally dries them is the revelation that for once he is alone, truly alone; ever since he had been tossed overboard, the voice has been silent. With this solace, he curls up into a little ball and falls asleep—a sleep wrought with nightmarish memories.

He is seven years old. He wakes from a peaceful sleep. It is the middle of the night. He wanders the house trying to discern the origin of the noise. He stops and listens. He hears it again, a faint, drawn-out moan. It is coming from his mother's room. He walks in that direction. He peeks into the room. His mother is naked and straddling a man who lies on his back. The man's eyes are closed in ecstasy. His mother, who is bouncing ecstatically up and down on the prone man, turns to him. She grins. She licks her crimson lips and winks. He watches as the man tightens his grip on his mother's hips and begins to convulse. A long moan of pleasure escapes his lips. It is his last, for the boy's mother leans forward and rips the man's throat out with her teeth. The dream shifts. He is five. He is playing in the back of the house. He falls asleep beneath a great olive tree west of the hut near the black swamp.

A noise wakes him. He opens his eyes and sees his mother throw something into the stagnant water. She looks around but does not see him, and makes her way back toward the small hut. He walks over to the pond. His mother told him numerous times to stay away from it, that it is dangerous but he is bested by curiosity. He stands at the edge of the moonlit waters, gazing into its murky depths. They were alive with a teeming horde of swimming shapes, the bobbing heads and flailing arms were alien and aberrant in a way scarcely to be expressed or consciously formulated. He hears a most detestably sticky noise as of some fiendish and unclean species of suction when, suddenly, a creature breaks the surface from below like a crab with pyramided fleshy rings or knots of thick, ropy stuff covered with feelers where a man's head should be, and wraps its tentacles around the boy's neck. He is half-dragged, half-sucked down into the unnamable abyss of the squalid, stagnant black mire.

The next thing that he remembers is his mother screaming at him as she slaps him across the face, "I told you to stay away from the water!"

He pulls away from her.

"I'm sorry, honey," she breathes, "Come to Mommy."

He walks timidly towards her and she pulls him to her breast, stroking his wet, slimy head.

He feels comforted by the words, the warm embrace, and her womanly scent.

"You know I love you the most," she croons. She puts her hands to the sides of his head and tilts his face upwards. Looking into his eyes she says 'I love you' once more.

"What's this?" she asks as she notices that he is becoming erect.

Embarrassed, he tries to pull away from her embrace.

"It's okay, honey," she breathes in his ear, "Totally natural. My boy is becoming a man." She says this almost as if with pride. Then a cloud glazes her eyes. He knows the look, has seen it many time in the eyes of the older boys before one of the 'games'.

"Come," she urges. She grasps his hand and drags him toward her bedroom.

Later that night, he tried to make sense of everything as he cried himself to sleep.

The man wakes with the dream bringing a question to his mind. "Who are you really?" he asks aloud.

An image flashes in his mind. Two fetuses entwined head-to-toe within each other's embrace. A pink sea surrounds them as they suckle on each other's penises.

I Am the Thing of the Idols. I Am the green, sticky spawn of the stars, the voice returns, *We...are one!*

The image changes as one of the twins begins to devour the other, the pink sea quickly turning red.

I am ravenous, my brother!

The man is stunned but knows the revelation to be true.

He had eaten his own brother! Even *in utero*, he had been a cannibal.

From this point on, he tries to ignore the fiendish buzzing, the incessant whispering of the hateful and unhuman voice as it continuously assaults him.

He languishes in the fleshy hell-the lonely, dark cell, so lonely that it could destroy the strongest of minds; the voice has infected his mind like a parasite, the only thing keeping him company. He knows that no one will ever understand what has brought him to this point. The voice is stronger and more pervasive then ever, and like his twin, the man is ravenous.

To sustain himself, he begins to gnaw on the walls of his prison. For the next few weeks-weeks that feel to him more like years-he eats, sleeps, and goes mad.

Chapter II

WAKE UP! IT *is time*.

As his eyes open, he feels his body being jerked to and fro. He is slammed into the wall of his cabin, and then thrown out of his cot and onto the hard, planked floor.

Soon. Soon! The voice whispers luridly in his mind. *He will be here in moments*.

Realizing that a storm is raging, the man pushes himself into a sitting position, then stands and makes his way the few feet to the small portal above the table. It is being pelted with rain and hail. He opens it.

Beyond the portal, the squall has grown in strength and transformed into a tempest-a force that knew the secrets of a man's heart and could tear his soul to shreds. The rage of the storm mirrors that which twists and writhes like a hungry worm in his mind.

There is a knock on his door.

Dinner has arrived.

"Please go away," the man begs of the voice. "Leave me alone. Please!"

Do not be a coward! Open the door and let him in, it is time.

He opens the door, and there stands the beautiful young man, a plate of steaming food in one hand, a small clay jar in the other and a wicked grin on his face.

He enters the cabin, and walks over to the small table. The man closes the door behind the boy and turns to watch as he sets the two items down, and then turns, and without uttering a word, drops his tunic to the floor.

A gift from the violent onslaught, the boy is like a beautiful, grotesque cherub.

His naked skin glows in the light of the oil lamp, his sandy blond hair tousled, his chest, muscular for his age with brown, coin-shaped nipples, his uncircumcised penis already half-hard and pointing right at him, his scrotum soft and smooth, making a mockery of the man's own deformed testicles.

No one deserves to be so beautiful, the voice taunts, *make him pay. You know how.*

He thinks of all that his suffering has caused him to lose—his innocence, his home, his sanity. All that remains is the voice and its determination to destroy him.

He grabs handfuls of the boy's fair hair, and pulls the ethereal face towards his own waiting mouth. His engorged tongue parts the boy's lips without resistance; it snakes into the pliant mouth, brushing across the smooth teeth, seeking out the warm pink tongue within. He then slowly retracts his own swollen tongue, enticing the smaller one of the boy to venture into his waiting maw. His teeth settle lightly, teasingly around the small pink muscle. His third arm slithers from beneath his robe.

The boy, his eyes shut, moans with desire and starts to gyrate against the hand, which wraps itself around his erect member and begins to stroke. As he gets more involved in the kiss, he reaches up and puts his small smooth hands over the older man's rough ones, which are still entangled in his hair. A moment goes by before he realizes that something is off. He lowers one of his hands to investigate what is going on at his crotch. He raises the hand again to explore the other two hands, which writhe and twist in his hair. He drops both hands and wedges them, palms out, against the man's chest. He tries to push away from the man. The teeth tighten on his tongue. The speed and urgency of the strokes increase and become rough. He realizes the he is trapped in the sinister embrace.

Do it! The voice urges, *Make him pay like all the others!*

He tries to drown it out, but it is of no use; the blood has abandoned his brain to collect in his erect tongue.

As the boy begins to ejaculate, the man simultaneously rips the tongue from his pubescent mouth, swallowing it, and tears his spurting member from its scrotum. The boy convulses; then goes slack in his strong grip. He gently lays the beautiful body, now spurting blood and oozing ichor, onto the hard wooden planks and climbs atop him. He begins to feed.

After gorging himself, he falls asleep.

When a sailor later finds the mutilated body of the cabin boy with the bloodied man snoring beside him, hot bile erupts from his churning gut leaving a burning trail up the pathways of his chest and throat. The acrid vomit explodes from his mouth, splattering his own sandaled-feet as well as the mutilated body of the dead cabin boy; melting and mingling with the pool of tacky, already congealing blood. The sound of his retching causes the man to roll over in his sleep, exposing his third arm, which flops down and lands in a pile of offal in the center of the carnage. Its clenched fist still grips a globule that looks suspiciously like a boy's penis. This new revelation invokes fresh vomiting from the sailor before he turns and runs from the cabin.

Several minutes later, he returns with a dozen men. The madman is sitting on the floor with his back propped against his cot. His third arm is feeding him the boy's cock.

They drag him to the outer deck and in a few moments one of them returns with Ol' Cap'n Obed.

Even in his crazed state, the man sees that something is off about the captain. He is naked except for a strange diadem on his narrow head. The surface of his body appears as if its peeling from some cutaneous disease. His watery blue eyes bulge; never to blink. Through long fat lips, he begins to mumble an incantation without nouns, but only verbs and pronouns. As he continues, the sailors strip off their clothing and join the chant.

Ol' Cap'n Obed's rambling voice scrapes and whispers on:

"Ph'nglui mglw'nafh Cthulhu R'lyeh wgah'nagl fhtagn!"

97

Then, with large heavily veined hands, he brings a flute to his thick drooping lips and begins to play demonic music.

As he plays, the naked sailors encircle him, becoming a flopping horde; mindless amorphous dancers. They lift the maniacal cannibal and throw him overboard into the mighty eddying and foaming of the brine.

Chapter I

He expected it would be a perilous journey yet still he heads for Tarshish refusing the order. By rebelling against the voice, he is desperately trying to hold on to the last shreds of his sanity.

As he boards the Philistine cargo boat, the gray wood planks—brittle under his sandaled feet—look like the skeletal remains of a beached whale. He notices the intricate hieroglyphics carved into the hull of the *Alert*—aquatic symbols such as fish, eels, octopi, crustations, mollusks, whales and the like; and certain sort of men, damnably human in general outline despite webbed hands and feet, shockingly wide and flabby lips, glassy bulging eyes—and other features less tasteful. He recognizes the depiction of Dagon, the Philistine Fish-God.

Burly men load freight onto the ship and pay him no notice. He does catch the eye of an epicene cabin boy who smiles and walks toward him.

"You look lost," he says, "Do you need help?"

"I'm not sure where I am supposed to go from here, where my cabin is." He shows the boy his pass.

"Looks like we will be neighbors," the boy replies, taking the man's satchel, "Follow me, I'll show you."

As they make their way into the belly of the ship, he studies the boy's graceful movements of the boy and arousal stirs within his mouth.

Yes, the voice intimates, *Beautiful*.

"Go away!" He curses beneath his breath.

"I'm sorry?" the boy glances over his shoulder at the strange, attractive man.

"Nothing," he replies, "I just have a painful cramp in my thigh."

"Oh," the boy says, his full lips stretching into a smile. "Here it is."

They arrive at a rough heavy door which the boy opens exposing a utilitarian cabin, bare except for a squat table, a chair, and a threadbare cot. Over the table a small mold-covered portal looks onto a sky that is just beginning to cloud over. He sets the man's bag on the bed.

"If you need anything, I am two doors down, on the right. Most of the mariners say that I have magic fingers; I could come back later and work that cramp for you," he states. To the man's surprise, the boy winks at him.

"Thank you. I think I will take you up on that. I need to get some rest first."

"I'll come back in two hours with some dinner, and some tallow to rub into your thigh." He smiles at the man and exits the cabin, closing the door behind him.

Perfect! The voice speaks up, when they are finally alone. *That was too easy.*

He curls up and drifts into a fitful sleep. The boy has triggered memories of his childhood, images that shift in and out of focus. He dreams.

The voice had started when he was twelve. He went to bed one evening smooth and had woken up the next morning with soft, downy hair under his arms (even the small, wing-like, third arm had this new growth) and around his groin. While exploring the short, wiry pubic hair, he had also found that what used to be a loose piece of skin beneath his penis was now heavy, swollen, and dangling. He stroked the bulging sack and squeezed it lightly discovering something that felt like a large olive. Intrigued by this find, he had prodded a little further counting three more of these 'olives'. He knew what this meant. He had often played Adam & Eve with some of the older boys from the nearby town of Joppa, and these boys' testicles had already dropped. What confused him was the fact that he had four of them where his playmates had always had only two.

Later, that same afternoon, the voice had come. He was playing Samson and Delilah with an older boy named Nephi. Because he was younger and a 'freak', he had always played the female in these games. After a few minutes of the familiar groping, Nephi had noticed the change in his playmate's organs.

"What's this?" he asked, cupping the younger boy's bulging scrotum, "Looks like it's time for a new game. Get down on your knees, Delilah, and put it in your mouth. Move up and down on it." While giving these instructions, Nephi had reached up and untied the leather strip that held his hair into place, letting it fall loosely around his shoulders.

"Don't worry," he said, "when my seed comes, just swallow it. Put it into your mind that you are swallowing a bunch of tiny fish. It'll be easy."

The boy, 'Delilah', following orders, dropped to his knees.

Nephi spread his tunic and withdrew a rather large red erection.

"Come on now; show Samson that you love him," Nephi had said, putting his hands on the back of the younger boy's head and guiding his mouth towards the rigid member.

From the boy's position on the ground, Nephi's penis had been at eye-level and looked like an angry red cobra ready to strike.

After a moment of hesitation, the boy had gripped Nephi's waist, and pulling him forward, had wrapped his mouth around the pulsating flesh. It squirmed around in his mouth, probing for his tonsils. Within moments, Nephi began to convulse and applied pressure with his hands, shoving the mouth all the way to the base of his engorged penis, gagging the boy. Thick, venomous liquid had exploded into his strained throat.

At the moment of Nephi's orgasm, two unexpected things had simultaneously happened. While his two normal hands still gripped Nephi's waist, Jonah's third arm, which had always hung limp and lifeless from his chest, twitched, then shot up between the legs of the older boy, his clenched fist entering Nephi's rectum, the force pushing the older boy's cock further into his throat.

Second, a voice, seemingly from nowhere and everywhere all at once, spoke.

Bite it. Rip it from its root.

He had not known the origin of the voice, but instinct had taken over. At Nephi's severed member had slid down his semen-lubricated throat, it caused a gusher of a different kind; blood erupted into his upturned face. Nephi screamed, then slovered and gibbered before dying. After removing the extra appendage from Nephi's ass, the boy had licked it clean of blood and feces. Then climbed atop his molester and started ripping hunks of hair from his head with his teeth.

"Samson, I have found the secret of thy strength," he mumbled; his mouth full of bloody scalp.

Later on the same long ago afternoon, he had cleaned up the mess and dragged Nephi's body to the swamp for his daemon siblings to feast on. Even at that young age, he had grasped the irony, for it had been Nephi who had first taunted him with lurid stories about his mother and her offspring. Some had called her "Black Widow," others a vampire. The grotesque tales had been shadowy and marvelous; of which grandmothers had whispered to children through the centuries. His mother was a legend.

That same evening, he had started to have second thoughts about the existence of the voice; thinking maybe he was going mad. Much had been happening; he had felt confused and violated. Maybe it had been nothing more than rage. Still, he was curious. He had decided to probe the question.

"Are you there?" he had asked the empty room around him.

"Hello? Who are you?"

I AM, a booming voice answered. He jumped. The voice had not been external, but somehow remained separate from his own thoughts. He had heard the stories of Moses and his experience with an unbodied voice, and Noah and Avraham and Yosef and Samuel.

"Who ... who's th ... there?" he had asked again.

I AM!

Again the voice. Then wicked laughter.

It told him that he was to go to Nineveh.

That dream drifts away and merges into a new one:

A naked woman lies on her back. Her stomach is swollen and covered in a fine sweat. She is screeching like an owl as she strains in childbirth. The woman is his mother. To her right stands a man. He knows the man as Amittai, his father. It dawns on him this dream is a memory of his own birth.

She pushes one last time, a scream escaping her throat. The babe is shoved into the world with a gush of warm blood and afterbirth; a third arm protruding from his gore-slick alabaster chest; a small broken wing.

Lilith brushes her sweaty hair from her brow, lifting the infant to her waiting mouth, and uses her teeth to sever the cord that connects them. Swallowing it, she puts the infant to her breast.

"My little dove," she whispers, "I will call you Jonah."

Amittai's Adam's apple bobs up and down, as he swallows nervously. Lilith turns to him and smiles. She then bares her sharp teeth and rips his throat out.

For Chuck Palahniuk

Alt. Hist. Anagram, Dec. 24th

Hidden,
we watch the fire
as, from the chimney, black
hooves appear. Cookies and milk for
Satan.

Stephen M. Wilson

candy

Earth, Moon, Sun, Stars, Planets
Quarks, Strings, Dark Matter ...

God takes a bite out of the
Milky Way

Christina's World

SHE DRANK THE water too fast then violently vomited, ejecting only clear bile for she hadn't eaten in several days. Lying at the pond's edge, she watched the sun rise through a hazy sky as silent sobs racked her body.

Later, she stripped and immersed herself. For an instant, she saw slack-clad legs in the murky depths.

"The world is yours, Christina, for the meek *shall* inherit the earth." Her father's voice boomed from the past.

She had been twelve and terrified when he'd purged her soul— not scared of the baptism itself, but that they might see her bleed.

Pinning a folded pillowcase to the inside of her panties made the procession to the river awkward—the wad of fabric had shifted up and down with each stride causing the tips of the straight-pins to prick her and blood to trickle down her thighs anyways. The friction had created another, more shameful, kind of dampness down there but she had endured, focusing her attention on Father's voice as he'd preached of the coming apocalypse.

Many a dark night, her father had taught fear and shame. No one, though, had taught her hope—hope was something she had recently learned on her own.

As she stepped to the bank, letting the water sluice away those bad memories as it trickled down her pale skin, her thoughts began to drift to earlier in the week. Though she was not ready to face *that* reality.

Looking at the small clapboard shack on the horizon, hunger was no longer her greatest concern.

"Please, God, let there be someone…anyone."

There was hope.

There was *always* hope for she had been so alone since the day she lay in the family field watching as the mushroom clouds reached for Heaven.

of winter *and* light
and the sun

all colors coalesce
into one and none

a promise
luminous
ominous
conflict diamonds
      drenched
      in blood

Delphi

Once, I was bitten by extremely
Fascinating
Electrical fire-creeps
Screaming!   Screaming!
As hungry boys with rigid cocks bloodied
A faerie.
I saw him
Silhouetted against
A sickle moon
In the black machinery of night
His cloven hooves
Shimmered in the dark waves
Of my memory
Then, he took flight—
Shooting through
The vestibule of my soul
Awe-stricken, the
Oracle wept.

siesta

Jesus slept.

AbOut the AuthOr

Stephen M. Wilson was Poetry Editor for *Abyss & Apex Magazine of Speculative Fiction* and also edited the spec poetry Twitterzine *microcosms* (@microcosms) and San Joaquin Delta College's literary magazine Artifact. Wilson spent 3+ years as Poetry Editor for *Doorways Magazine* and co editor of the Science Fiction Poetry Association's annual Dwarf Stars Award anthology. He's had several poems nominated for the Rhysling Award and a handful for the Dwarf Stars Award (including a win in 2011). His first book *Dark Duet*, a collaboration with multi-Bram Stoker Award winner Linda D. Addison, is available from Necon E-Books. Wilson lived in Stockton, CA with his partner and two dogs. More at: http://speceditor666.livejournal.com.

Linda D. Addison has won three HWA Bram Stoker Award®. Catch her latest work in *Dark Duet*, a collaborative book of poetry and HWA Bram Stoker Award® finalist, written with Stephen M. Wilson and *Four Elements*, collection with Rain Graves, Charlee Jacob and Marge Simon (Bad Moon Books); *High Stakes* anthology (Evil Jester Press). She is a member of HWA, CITH, SFWA, and SFPA. Keep up with her at www.lindaaddison.com.

www.ingramcontent.com/pod-product-compliance
Lightning Source LLC
LaVergne TN
LVHW041159080426
835511LV00006B/672